Write on Time!

*Prompt & Perfect Pitch Angles
That Get Media Attention*

By
MICHELBY L. WHITEHEAD

Write on Time!
Prompt & Perfect Pitch Angles That Get Media Attention

www.pressbeyondmeasure.com

Copyright © 2021 by Michelby L. Whitehead of Michelby & Co, LLC

Without limiting the rights under copyright above, no part of this publication may be reproduced, stored in or introduced into a retrieval system, or transmitted, in any form, or by means (electrical, mechanical, photocopying, recording, or otherwise), without the prior written permission of both the copyright owner and the publisher of the book.

ISBN # 978-0-578-81297-7
Published by Michelby & Co, LLC

Printed in the United States of America

Formatting by Alandria Lloyd- The Writer's Block LLC
Cover Design by Allison Arnett
Editing by Tamika L. Sims

This book is available at quantity discounts for bulk purchases. For information, please email hello@michelby.com .

What People Are Saying About...

CoCo | CURATOR

I got off the phone with her and I got my entire life! As a creative, I've been a bit overwhelmed for too long and after this conversation, I'm very clear about what I need to do and how to go about it. If you need help with direction in your career or your brand, reach out to Michelby! She's truly gifted and inspirational. I'm still speechless!

Candice W.

Comedian & Content Creator

Gotta give a testimonial to the one and only Michelby CoCo Whitehead! Sis came through with the BOMB strategy session today and it has REALLY helped me figure out WTF I am doing. I now have purpose, and drive, and dare I say, passion! I've spent the last four months in limbo, and it feels amazing to feel like I sort of know what I want to do and why. Thank CoCo! Xoxoxo... Bloggers/media professionals... contact her.

She knows her stuff (But have a check ready. She's not free).

Lisa F.
Lifestyle Blogger

I was Michelby's client for an online sales campaign. In our partnership, Michelby displayed a level of professionalism, wit, and creative thought that is quite rare among boutique agencies. Her writing and research skills are truly phenomenal! I was in need of a pitch to a major brand. She wrote and delivered a remarkable pitch letter that landed the brand partnership that I was yearning for.

Victoria R.
Event Designer

When I think of media and public relations, Michelby, is always top of mind. No matter if it's a member of her celebrity clientele or an up and coming author or speaker, she serves with a heart-centered passion and focus. If you are looking for someone to take your brand or business to the next level, she is your girl.

Tamika S.
Author Coach

Michelby CoCo Whitehead is the real deal! When I say, the 90-minute consult set me on fire! Excellence all the way around, if you are looking for a publicist or someone to help you move in the right direction. Do not hesitate to contact this Queen. When I got off the conference call, I had to rethink everything I thought I knew about my own company! If you're not sure how to market on social media, or what a media kit is, contact her! She poured all she had in me and I have moved leaps and bounds. Michelby CoCo Whitehead I truly appreciate your honesty and empowerment!

Latisha A.
Life Coach

Attending Michelby's "I Need Business Besties Brunch" was a great experience for me. I'd moved to New Orleans and was looking for an opportunity to learn from other businesswomen and do a bit of networking. The speakers were from different states with various backgrounds, and they were all engaging and knowledgeable. Not only did I meet new women I've continued to stay in touch with, but I connected with a few women whom I've been friends with via social media.

For me, the best part about the brunch was the information I received from the speakers. There was something shared that no matter what industry you were in, someone in the audience could relate to it. Someone could use it. Someone could benefit from it. And, to top it off, I met THE Mia X! Good food. Good music. Good connections. I'm looking forward to CoCo's next curated event.

> Joyce K.
> Speaker & Author

Working with CoCo was one of the best business decisions I've made! Not only is she knowledgeable, creative, and relatable, Michelby knows how to cultivate meaningful relationships and has a plethora of resources.

> Sharlonda P.
> Public Health Officer

To my grandmother Ms. Helen Elizabeth Boyd Welch. You told me I was influential, and you ain't never lied. I love you!

To my Aunt Susan, may God restore your health tenfold.

Mom & Dad, thank you for giving me a foundation in God and a princess lifestyle!

Marquia, you're the drill sergeant and life coach I didn't ask for but need. Dream, you're an angel in disguise. Shai Henry, you're simply the BEST!

Nola and Keba, fly high!

To all my siblings, aunts, uncles, nieces, nephews, godchildren, cousins, and anyone I consider family or a friend, thank you!

Nikki Walton, Darla Montgomery, Jacque Reid, Lila Brown, Saptosa Foster, Monchiere Jones, and Lisa Jackson, thank you for being mentors.

Thanks to my brilliant assistant Ayanna.

My biz bestie Ambir, I see you.

And to my dog (dawg) Ace.

-MLW

Contents

Foreword 1

Section 1: Understanding Public Relations 3

Section 2: Communication Without Clarity Is Confusion 11

Section 3: Now That's A Bad Pitch 21

Section 4: Waiting On Your Yes! 25

Section 5: They Said Yes To Press, Now What? 29

Section 6: Live From The Living Room 35

Section 7: Pitch Angles For You 39

Section 8: Media Jargon Glossary 49

About The Author 53

Tools You Can Use 55

FOREWORD

When it comes to hiring a publicist, relationships are everything. What you're paying for is contacts and connections and CoCo is a beast at building relationships that result in profitable partnerships.

I've had the privilege of working with CoCo on several projects over the last few years including press for local events, media coverage for digital events, and even landing gigs on international platforms! I've truly benefited from being connected to her and she is the PLUG when it comes to securing valuable media placements.

Her wealth of experience and abundance of knowledge makes her the perfect person to pen this book. She is truly a gem and shares many of her success secrets within these pages. From her experience working with and writing for national publications to her time working with influencers and celebrities, she's able to share all of her lessons learned, and mistakes made that can help you jumpstart your career and get the word out about your hard work!

I love the way she breaks down publicity and media in layman's terms that even a beginner can digest. She offers tips, tricks, and tools to navigate every aspect of the pitching process, whether you want to hire a publicist or do it yourself.

From clarifying your message to presenting your work to media contacts, she is gifting you with the tools you need to take PR into your own hands.

You are surely in for a treat with this read. Sit back, take notes, and prepare to apply all of your lessons learned.

Kudos to you, CoCo, and congratulations on a job well done!

Koereyelle DuBose,
Serial Entrepreneur, Educator + Founder of WERK University

Section 1

UNDERSTANDING PUBLIC RELATIONS

Myths, Mindsets, & Mistakes

What exactly is PR?

This is a great question that potential clients rarely ask. When we think we know something, we don't go deeper to get more information; that's human nature.

First things first, I am NOT a PR! The term we use in this century (and have been using for *quite* some time) is publicist. Press rep hasn't been on fleek for ages, and press agent was used back in PT Barnum's heyday when he was swindling people at the circus with surreal acts.

Public relations is not solely social media posts, memes, or passing out flyers. These things can aid in an individual or organization's public relations efforts, but they should never be singled out as public relations.

According to the Public Relations Society of America, public relations, or PR, is "a strategic communication process that builds mutually beneficial relationships between organizations and their publics."

Pretty simple definition. However, the part that can make public relations difficult to grasp, is not understanding how to identify your publics. Your publics are the people you serve, as well as the people who you wish to favorably influence.

Take a motivational speaker for example. The people he or she currently serves can range from elementary students to recovering substance abusers. Ideally, this speaker should see organizations such as Mothers Against Drunk Driving and the Department of Juvenile Justice as members of its "publics." Having such relationships can position this motivational speaker as the go-to person.

No matter the industry you are in, you have a public to cater to, maybe several. Once you have identified who these groups are, you can determine how to reach them through the media.

With that being said, the duration of this book will focus on providing education on the importance of media coverage, and actionable steps to secure it for your brand, business, or organization.

Advertising Vs. Earned Media

Media can be paid for, or it can cost absolutely nothing! When you see a full-page ad in Essence magazine for Rihanna's Fenty Cosmetics, that is advertising. On the flip side, an article in Essence Magazine showcasing Fenty Face as one of the ten best foundations to wear this summer is a form of earned media.

Anyone with a budget can get advertising, but to have a prestigious media outlet take the time to interview you, or write about your products and services is priceless, and is seen as a stamp of approval. Ultimately, this connects you to the audiences you wish to expose to your brand. The more eyes on your brand, the more opportunities you attract. Opportunities can range from increased sales to speaking on huge platforms and even becoming a brand ambassador with corporate sponsorship.

So PR is like marketing?

Although they complement each other, they are not the same. Marketing is the action or business of promoting and selling products or services, including market research and advertising.

As mentioned earlier, PR focuses on crafting the right brand message and emotions the consumer or intended audience is to feel through written, verbal, and visual communication.

What can a publicist do for me?

Hiring a publicist can be a rather indispensable investment for your big brand or small business. Ultimately, the job of a publicist is to make an individual, product, or organization stand out in its industry and always be seen as the best thing since sliced bread! When you hire a publicist, you are trusting this person to position your brand with the right opportunities for more visibility.

Let me give you an example, let's say you are a retired school teacher who creates learning materials for kids. If you hire a publicist to help you secure press placements, then I PRAY your publicist is not wasting time sending pitch emails to *Bossip*.

Well, what's wrong with Bossip, Michelby?

For this scenario, everything is wrong with it. While the lovely editors at Bossip do a fantastic job of covering celebrity news, reality shows, and pop culture in general, a pitch about science flashcards has no value for that outlet. Nine times out of ten, you won't even receive a "sorry, we're not interested" response because one should already know the type of content the outlet desires. Decision-makers in the media can't waste minutes explaining something you should have already researched.

Now, if your publicist manages to get this product into the hands of an influencer who is a parent, like Ciara or Russell Wilson, then pitching to Bossip from that angle makes all the sense in the world.

Got it? Great! Let's clear up another myth that may be puzzling you.

I need to work with a celebrity publicist

We have a tendency to automatically associate publicists with paparazzi lights, red carpets, and a Kardashian lifestyle. In actuality, the Red Cross and your local sanitation company scream everything but the glamorous life, and yet they have a communications team handling their public image.

It is not a must that you work with a celebrity publicist. Most people who work in public relations have a niche, and sometimes they only operate best in that area of genius. Find a publicist that has a proven track record of excellence securing the type of media placements and opportunities that are RELEVANT TO YOUR GOALS.

Beyonce' can be on the cover of *Time* or *Rolling Stone* with ease. She's the wife of a billionaire who is possibly the greatest rapper alive and an international pop star who constantly sets trends. These publicity opportunities are in alignment with her brand and attainable for **her**. It would be silly to think you NEED to work with her publicist, Yvette Noel-Schure when your goal is to spread awareness of your online boutique. Instead, retain a reputable publicist who is well-versed in fashion PR so that you can be featured in articles via *Vogue*, *Fashion Bomb Daily*, or *Essence*.

It can't be that hard. Maybe I can pitch myself for interviews and feature stories...

Positive thinking will get you everywhere when you're also prepared! Like the old saying goes, "Prior planning prevents poor performance."

Getting media outlets to pay attention to you is totally achievable if you can position yourself to be an important voice in your industry. I will not tell you that it is easy. However, it gets easier with time. Luckily, you'll have an advantage over your competitors because I'm sharing all the tactics and resources I've used to get my clients seen on platforms like BET, Essence Festival, Revolt, and more.

You want press, and you can get it NOW with my coaching. Let's get this party started!

Section 2

COMMUNICATION WITHOUT CLARITY IS CONFUSION

I love Chinese food. It's yummy and it gives me words of wisdom when I think I'm grown and know everything there is to know about life. Last year, one of my fortune cookies threw shade when I was having a serious case of writer's block.

The cookie stated: *Good writing is clear thinking made visible.*

For a few days, I recall looking at the little slip of paper like it was an overdue bill— aggravating and serving absolutely no purpose. Then one day I took a break from blogging and it all made sense.

Good writing IS clear thinking made visible!

You can't convey an idea on paper, or verbally until YOU understand what the heck it is you're trying to say. You know, like when your five-year-old comes into the kitchen whining as a second language to convey hunger, and you tell her, "Use your words!"

The same goes for pitching media. The more concise and confident you are about what you're saying, the easier it is for any decision-maker to see why your story deserves to be publicized on that platform.

Get your favorite pen and pad; this is where the lesson begins.

Don't Pitch a Thing Until You Do This!

Get crystal clear on your message

Plainly define the "thing" you want the media to talk about. Is it your weight loss journey? Did you open a new business? Are you collecting gently used coats for the local homeless shelter? Are you advocating for racial equality in your city? The narrative you convey should be in alignment with the end result you're seeking.

Assess the story's newsworthiness

Why should anyone care? That is a valid question that should not offend you. Your local news station and major outlets only want to cover stories that will spark the interest of those tuning in. Figure out what makes your story interesting or impressive and run with it. Keep in mind that "newsworthy" is determined by the story's news values. News values influence the selection and presentation of events that are published as news. New values include the following:

- Timeliness- You must write and submit pitches on time, hence this book's title! Who wants to read about the church Easter egg hunt in July?
- Impact- How many people were affected? How quickly does it work?
- Proximity- The closer it hits home, the more newsworthy.
- Prominence- Are there any important or well-known people involved?
- Relevance- Is this a current topic of convo?
- Oddity- How rare or special is it?
- Conflict- Is there a problem or issue at hand?

- Human Interest- What experiences can people connect with? What emotions will it bring forth? Can the outlet's audience empathize?
- Extremes/Superlatives- Is it the worst? Is it the first? Is it the most heroic? Give us some adjectives!
- Scandal- Can we sip tea on this? Is there any drama?

Determine what you ultimately want to gain from media exposure.

No one should be participating in interviews for kicks. The value of media visibility is absolutely priceless, and it would be insane to take it for granted should you land an opportunity. Ask yourself: *What do I hope to gain from this?*

Sharing your message should result in *something*, but it's up to you to know what that something is. Here's a scenario to ponder. I had a client who was the mother of an autistic child in high school. She penned a best-selling book on methods she used to prepare her son for college, elaborating on the naysaying from her son's high school administrators who believed he would never get accepted. She expressed to me that her goal was to get more speaking engagements on autism; therefore, she was in need of high-profile publicity to heighten the public's awareness of her prowess.

The only way to measure the effectiveness of leveraged press is to know what your end result is. (Notice I said leveraged press; securing it isn't enough). If you don't know the end goal, then how can you conclude if your efforts were successful or not?

"Get your ask together." That's what Lucinda Cross says in her book, *The Big Ask*. Your pitch email should not leave the reader wondering why you wrote to him or her. Monique Malcolm of the Pimp Your Brilliance podcast also agrees. To be on her show, she stresses that potential guests have the following in their pitch email to get a "yes."

- Who you are
- What you do
- Why you do it and why people should care
- How you'll bring value to the media platform
- The expert topics you can speak on

- Links to past interviews (audio or written) so the host can get an idea of what you're workin' with!

If you don't have links to showcase, I would suggest taking the initiative to shoot a decent video, (two minutes is sufficient), displaying your competence on the subject matter. Don't let one curable hiccup stop you from pitching.

Earning more money is another reason entrepreneurs seek media attention. Now, the money is not going to fall from Heaven because you participated in an interview.. Again, you must LEVERAGE! To get to the coins, one should utilize earned media to:

- Generate more leads
- Increase speaking engagements
- Get participation in a call-to-action
- Increase social media followers
- Be seen as a reputable industry expert

If your goal is to sell a product or service, then PLEASE have it prominently displayed on your website and ready for purchase. I guarantee that after you've been heard on a podcast or seen in print or television, people will look you up. Why not have something readily available that they can purchase, or at minimum, a clever lead magnet to get them to join your mailing list?

> **#WriteOnTimeTip**
>
> Create a calendar of special holidays that apply to your industry so that you can center your pitch around hot topics in a timely fashion!

Identify the media outlets that are best suited to convey your message

Imagine holding a conversation with a customer service rep for 60 minutes about the poor Wi-Fi connection you're experiencing, only to be told you've dialed the wrong internet company…

I wish I could insert a gif of Mike Tyson, George Foreman, and Muhammad Ali all fighting the air here!

I guarantee you this is the anger you will experience should you waste time pitching outlets that have no benefit to your overall agenda. To avoid this from happening, make a potential list of outlets you're interested in and evaluate if they are the right platforms to position your message. Here's what you need to consider:

- Relevance of your message to its audience
- Audience size
- Audience demographics
- Credibility and public perception of the outlet

Gather all your ammunition for a killer pitch email

You are now ready to get your pitch on! To do this the right way, you'll need these important assets on deck:

- A press release or one-sheet
  - This helps the editor or assigned writer craft your story with the narrative you hope to convey
- Professional hi-resolution images, especially a headshot
- Any relevant links that will help sell the story
- Up-to-date contact information.

I'm sure you have heard of a media kit, and are probably wondering why I didn't mention it in the list. The reason I excluded it from the list is because you're probably just starting to pursue media opportunities; therefore, you have no media clips to create a media kit. In the meantime, you can make a one-sheet, a single-page document that summarizes your brand for publicity purposes.

Section 3

NOW THAT'S A BAD PITCH

Contrary to popular belief, a good press release or pitch email is more than spelling the words correctly. This masterpiece you're writing will be your first impression. It is your chance to state why your brand or business should be seen or heard on a particular media platform. Running spell check and looking for proper use of semicolons isn't enough. There are other critical factors that can make or break your chances of getting press.

If your messages have been left on read by someone you thought had an interest in building a relationship, then you know what it feels like to be ghosted. What makes it even more difficult is not getting closure from the other party—the underlying reason for the rejection.

I'm no relationship guru like Steve Harvey, but I can tell you why your pitches are being rejected by the media outlets you adore. And when you know better, you can pitch better and be celebrated by the right outlets! This next section may hurt, but you'll appreciate me for it when the media inquiries start flooding your inbox.

5 Reasons Decision Makers Ditch Your Pitch

Your writing is trash

Many stories are overlooked because the request is hard to understand or simply isn't up to par. A journalist's time is limited, so grabbing his or her attention with well-written communication is a must. Make sure the first paragraph contains the who and what, but ultimately *why* his or her audience needs to see you on the platform.

You got the wrong one, baby

A great way to irritate a journalist or blogger is to send pitches that are totally irrelevant to what he or she writes about. In some cases, the wrong journalist will forward it to the right person on staff, but as mentioned, time is limited in the newsroom, so don't always count on that to happen. In addition to that, your contact may not work there anymore.

> #### #WriteOnTimeTip
>
> Unless you're trying to get in a holiday gift guide, never pitch in regards to what you sell. Focus on how you solve a certain problem and how that expertise will benefit the outlet's audience.

You're giving a snooze

So, you're having a launch... What's new? Figure out how to make what you're doing a big deal, but in an **authentic way, not in a sensational way**. For example, many people are launching nonprofit organizations, but wouldn't it be interesting to know the founder overcame some obstacle, like only having a 6th-grade education? Transparency is what allows people to connect with you. Find what sets your story apart from the rest and pitch from that angle. If you're ashamed of your story, then you can't relish in the glory.

You don't know how to play politics

Be extra polite when trying to secure press. Greet journalists and editors properly in email by their name; a general greeting screams that you are pitching the story to multiple outlets. Even if you are, it shouldn't be obvious! Also, mention facts about the outlet's audience that coincides with why you would be the perfect person to feature.

Section 4

WAITING ON YOUR YES!

Press Beyond Measure is my PR coaching program for entrepreneurs. In addition to a free PR webinar training every month, I coach clients through the pitch process and give the leads on media opportunities.

Once Rhonda Reporter reads a pitch I've helped your craft, you'll receive a response. What I cannot do is clear Rhonda's schedule and make her open the pitch email the instant you send it.

As I previously mentioned, traditional and digital media rooms are BUSY. Consider that you are not the only person vying for this outlet's attention, and don't get offended because you haven't gotten a response in lightning speed. Simply follow up with another email or phone call.

Remember that there is a fine line between checking on the status of something and being a nuisance. Keep reading; I've got a solution for that!

Check out other options

You need to treat this pitching thing like dating. Keep pursuing outlets until someone commits to allowing you to tell your story. I'll give you an example.

For whatever reason, a popular site for millennial women was taking entirely too long to run my client's interview that had been conducted in May. Summer was about to end and I decided to keep pitching to similar outlets with the same audience. Unless you've signed some type of agreement stating such, there's no rule that says only one outlet can run your story.

Did I mention that I was also a freelance writer? One of my Facebook friends released a coloring book for female entrepreneurs. Because coloring is a proven therapeutic stress reliever, I thought it would make a great story for my readers at Curly Nikki, a lifestyle digital platform that focuses on natural hair and mental health for Black women. Once the story went live on the site, a writer at Black Enterprise saw it and reached out to my Facebook friend to interview her about the EXACT thing I wrote about.

So, again, it's okay to slide into other editors' and reporters' DM until you get what you came for—PRESS, PRESS, PRESS!

Sometimes email isn't enough

If the pandemic of 2020 has taught me anything, I've been forced to remember this: You've got to be more proactive than you've ever been! This includes your efforts to build relationships with media professionals.

Did you know that I built my career in the bayou region of south Louisiana? (I know, go ahead and clutch your imaginary pearls). One side of my family is from New Orleans and the other is spread through Acadiana, particularly Franklin and Jeanerette, Louisiana. When I realized that being a successful publicist was heavily based on relationships, I concluded that I could have a thriving career while enjoying my family and the best food in the world right where I grew up. I didn't worry about moving to New York or Los Angeles because I knew that the internet was my key to building influence as an expert in public relations. If I do move, it'll be because I want to, not because my success depends on it.

> **#WriteOnTimeTip**
>
> You can find the right person to pitch by scanning the credits of a print magazine.

I strongly advise you to get out of your comfort zone and start a dialogue with people who work at local and national media outlets. How do you get in touch with them? Social media, of course! Every writer, reporter, and editor has a preferred social media platform they enjoy posting on.

Whether it's LinkedIn, Facebook, Instagram, or Twitter, these people are more accessible than you think and they are always on the hunt for awesome stories to cover.. So in turn, it would be in your best interest to talk about your brand or business more on social media and build relationships.

Section 5

THEY SAID YES TO PRESS, NOW WHAT?

There's More To An Interview Than Answering The Questions

Talking points for the win

Securing clients on the Tom Joyner Morning Show is something that I will always be proud of because I grew up listening to it. Each and every morning from kindergarten to high school, my parents, grandmother, and the school bus drivers were always tuned in to "the hardest working man in show business." This morning ritual continued for me in college and life after because the crew was *hee-larious*, even when it was time to be serious!

Because of this, I made sure to prepare my clients with talking points for those moments when Tom and his co-hosts would go off script and say something crazy. It's easy to get sidetracked in an interview; whether it's by the interviewer, or getting flustered by your own nervousness. This is why talking points are so important.

> **#WriteOnTimeTip**
>
> If your goal is to publicize your business or personal brand, having an elevator pitch makes the creation of talking points easier.

Talking points are a set of clear, easy to remember phrases that outline the vital parts of your message. No matter if you're going on local or national television, talking points are a game-changer. Once you determine what those statements need to be, submit them to the person who confirmed your interview. This will help him or her formulate the questions that will be asked, or the story in general if it's for print. If your interview is for television, radio, or podcast, then you'll already have an idea of what questions will be asked and how you should answer them.

Preparing for your moment on the small screen

I think anyone with a pulse enjoyed the episode of *Martin* where he convinced the gang to head to Hollywood so he could be a guest on the Varnell Hill Show. We can also agree that he was NOT the least bit prepared to be on a nationally syndicated live talk show.

Martin approached this "opportunity" wrong from every angle. Actually having someone from the media outlet confirm you as a guest is always protocol; you don't show up in the greenroom. These days, the same goes for social media. Unless you have the green light to do so, don't post that you're a guest on a platform. Moreover, if Martin's off-camera goof-ups weren't enough, he certainly made up for them on camera! He may have been a radio star, but he definitely could have used some media training for his television debut. Jodeci deserved so much more than a rendition of "Knick Knack Patty Wack Give a Dog a Bone."

I trust that you won't be as disruptive as Martin when you get your big opportunity. But just in case you've been inspired by his antics, consider these tips for a successful TV segment:

- **Ask for sample questions and practice your responses.** Remember to submit your talking points as well because the questions will piggyback off them. We don't have time for rambling; get the facts out while you have this golden moment to be seen by the masses. Again, talking points make the interview flow easier for both parties.

- **Video record yourself.** You need to see how your body language and posture translates on film. This gives you a chance to make the necessary corrections BEFORE your big day

- **Talk to the interviewer, not the camera.** A television interview is merely a conversation that happens to be captured on film—that's it! The interviewer is who you should be making eye contact with and talking to. Unless there is something to convey directly to those who are watching, you should NEVER talk to the camera. For example, "Please show your support by donating coats next Saturday" is acceptable to say to the camera at the end of your segment. Other than that, talk to the person who is talking to you so you don't look like a weirdo.

- **Actually, listen to the interviewer.** This sounds like a dumb statement on the surface, but you wouldn't believe how many times I've seen interviewees excessively nod like Bobbleheads and smile throughout the segment for no apparent reason! It's so awful to watch, and the people doing it don't seem to realize it. My guess is that these folks are typically nervous when speaking publicly, so they do it to appear confident and present in the moment. This doesn't make one look confident—it looks crazy! This is why I stress the importance of practicing the talking points and recording yourself.

Section 6

LIVE FROM THE LIVING ROOM

Swizz Beats and Timbaland gave us Verzuz while the medical industry provided telehealth during the Coronavirus pandemic. With the exception of voting, everything is becoming an online experience. Virtual interviews are certainly not new, but they are more popular than ever now.

The biggest media outlets have had no choice but to meet people where they are. The need to conduct interviews in a sophisticated 50-story building with posh furniture overlooking Manhattan or Los Angeles is no longer necessary.

On the flip side of things, this new normal has taken the pressure off smaller outlets to bring out the bells and whistles when competing for coverage against bigger outlets. In fact, Yvette Noel-Schure (you have to say her whole name every time; anything else doesn't flow right) said that when the pandemic hit, she made an executive decision to have Chloe and Halle, Beyonce's proteges, do a press junket inclusive to smaller entertainment outlets. Her rationale is that in a national pandemic, no stone should be left unturned to publicize a project, and she's right.

The rules for virtual and in-studio interviews are pretty much the same, except in this case, it is necessary to talk to the camera at all times. Another concern will be setting up a space that is conducive to providing a great interview.

Consider the SLAP acronym when setting up your personal studio:

Sound

Don't let your beeping smoke detector make you look like an amateur... Change the batteries before your interview.

Find a spot that has zero noise interference. If you will be recording from home and have no control of things such as nearby traffic, neighbors, and lawnmowers, then find another location such as a private room at your local library.

> **#WriteOnTimeTip**
>
> Your bathroom shower curtain is not a backdrop or a step and repeat banner. A virtual background or a cor-ner area with minimal wall decor are better options.

Moreover, be conscious of your microphone when it's NOT your turn to speak. You don't want to be heard snickering, belching, or mumbling under your breath. It's embarrassing!

Lighting

There's only so much editing can do. The more natural light in the room, the better. But since you can't always predict the weather, make sure the light fixtures in the room are flattering to you, especially if you plan on wearing makeup. Beat your face for the practice run to see exactly how you'll look because your foundation and concealer may not be the match you thought it was.

Angles

You don't want to be a talking, floating head on film. Give the interview a test run to discover the best angles to position your laptop or mobile device. Also, keep in mind that the way you show up on Facetime isn't necessarily how you'll look on Instagram Live or any other platform.

People

Put your people in place for the big day. That means sending the baby to a sitter to avoid sudden hunger cries and having your tech-savvy friend on deck to help if you still don't know what you're doing.

Section 7

PITCH ANGLES FOR YOU

Before we got to this chapter, I had to teach you a thing or two about public relations and pitching in particular. There's no way I'd give you pitch angles without teaching you the art of *how* to pitch. I mean, I do have integrity!

Sometimes, your brand or business will not have anything going on that is wildly exciting or considered breaking news. AND THAT IS PERFECTLY OKAY. However, your expertise and how it helps your public is always something to talk about.

Without further ado, here is what you've been waiting for—prompt and perfect pitch angles that get media attention. I've also included worksheets at the end of the book so you can plan your pitches like a pro!

Fashionistas

- Recaps of the best and worst outfits from award shows
- Unconventional wedding looks
- Chic thrift store finds for corporate looks
- How to camouflage "problem areas"
- Trends for prom

Food & Beverage Experts

- Tasty vegan dishes for the holidays
- National Chocolate Day
- Easy meals even dad can cook
- Wine tasting for beginners
- Food festivals to attend

Empowerment & Ministry

- Confronting imposter syndrome and restoring confidence

#WriteOnTimeTip

Newsjacking is a great way to submit timely, relevant pitches to the media!

- Transitioning from prison to the free world
- The pitfalls of Superwoman syndrome
- Forgiving yourself
- International Women's Day

Money Experts

- Student loan payback strategy that won't cause you to live like a pauper
- Understanding stocks and investments
- Side hustles from home that generate big bucks
- Tackling debt after divorce
- Building credit with no credit

Travel Experts

- Packing for extended vacations like a pro
- International honeymoon hacks
- Myth busters on obtaining a passport
- Avoiding travel agent scams
- How to take blog-worthy pics on trips

Health & Wellness Experts

- National Diabetes Month

- Caring for disabled loved ones
- Tips for geriatric pregnancy
- Choosing a cosmetic surgeon
- Yoga and meditation for widows

Legal Experts

- How to protect your inheritance
- Understanding music contracts
- Representing oneself in court
- Signs you may have been fired illegally
- Copyrights for creatives

Makeup Artists

- Glam face in 10 minutes
- Beauty product must-haves for women over 50
- Contouring like a pro
- Techniques for hiding raccoon eyes and other flaws
- Cosmetics for acne-prone skin

Hair Stylists

- Modern twists on 90s looks

- Natural hair products from the kitchen
- Hair loss solutions
- Making money outside of the salon
- Proper installment of a lacefront wig

Realtors

- Credit report mishaps that hinder homeownership
- Making your home appraisal profitable
- First-time homebuyer's program
- Why family units are a smart investment
- How to rock your next open house

Business Consultants

- Scaling business in 6 months or less
- How to get government contracts
- Finding the right business coach
- Systems needed to run a professional operation from home
- Structuring your non-profit

Social Media Consultants

- Getting content from Clubhouse
- Leveraging Tik Tok for online fundraising
- Guerilla marketing for authors
- Hashtag do's and don'ts
- Separating your personal brand from the professional

Mental Health

- Alternative treatments for depression
- Mental health awareness for entrepreneurs
- Preventing burnout and stress in overachievers
- Overcoming emotional abuse from childhood
- Coping with miscarriage and abortion

Love & Relationship Experts

- Dating after 40
- Discovering your love language
- Signs your partner isn't pleased in the bedroom
- Finding love online
- Polygamy in the new millennium

Parenting Experts

- National Adoption Month
- Making your blended family work
- Homeschooling in a pandemic
- Recognizing middle child syndrome
- Playdates for deaf toddlers

CBD Industry

- Healing benefits of hemp
- CBD for stressed-out moms
- Internet marketing for CBD brands
- Finding funding for your hemp business
- FDA regulations of cannabis products to know

Techies

- Components of a winning pitch deck
- Inspirational Garrett A. Morgan quotes every inventor should live by
- Cool gadgets for office executives
- The future of STEM in communities of color
- Building an app worth downloading

HR Experts

- Incorporating diversity and inclusion into company culture
- Signs you may have been illegally fired
- Networking on LinkedIn with no job experience
- Recruiting and retention for nonprofits
- Understanding 401K

Educators

- Finding funding to support auxiliary clubs
- Leadership tips for new administrative professionals
- Building rapport with problematic parents
- Virtual tutoring as a side hustle
- Support for non-traditional college students

Gamers

- Creating the perfect at-home gaming setup
- New product reviews
- Amplifying your social media presence
- Getting paid to play video games

- Top gaming conventions to attend

Photographers

- Easy editing even grandma can grasp
- Hacks for amazing photos with your smartphone
- Becoming a celebrity photography
- Curating a polished Instagram feed
- Tips for the camera shy

Plus-Size Influencers

- Breaking into full-figured modeling
- Working out while keeping your curves
- Building an online community
- Partnering with high-end brands for charitable causes
- Social media monetization with less than 10K followers

Animal Lovers

- Training your dog in 30 days
- Choosing the right veterinarian

- Home remedies for fleas
- Grooming on a budget
- Myths about microchips

Music Lovers

- New album reviews and listening parties
- James Brown's influence on hip-hop culture
- Things to consider when choosing artist management
- Setting up a recording studio at home
- National DJ Day

Section 8

MEDIA JARGON GLOSSARY

Every industry has jargon that sounds like gibberish to those unaware of it. Here are a few common words that you will hear as you pursue press and media opportunities for your brand or business:

Agenda-setting- Ability of the media to tell people what and whom to talk or think about

B-roll- Extra footage captured to enrich the story you're telling and to have greater flexibility when editing. It can include additional video footage, still photographs, animation, or other graphic elements

Beat- A particular topic or subject area that a journalist covers

Call time- The time the cast and crew of a production needs to be on the set and ready to work

HARO- Short for Help a Reporter Out, connects journalists seeking expertise on a particular subject to those who can provide the expertise

Managing editor- Senior member of a publication's management team who reports directly to the editor-in-chief and oversees all aspects of the publication

Media- Plural form of medium

Media kit- Also known as a press kit; a packaged set of promotional materials, such as photographs and background information for distribution to the media before the release of a new product or upcoming event. Because time is of the essence, many PR professionals distribute EPKs (electronic press kits) for their clients

Media savvy- Able to understand how the media works and ability to use media to one's advantage

Medium- Singular form of media, the term usually describes individual forms such as radio, television, etc.

Newsjacking- The practice of taking advantage of current events, trending topics, or news stories in such to promote or advertise one's product or brand

One sheet- Single document that summarizes a product for publicity

Photo-op- Short for photograph opportunity; an arranged opportunity to take a photograph of a notable person or event

Press release- A written communication sent to members of the media for the purpose of announcing something that is newsworthy, or of value, to its audience. It should provide reporters with the basic information needed to develop a feature story

Primetime - The part of a radio or television schedule expected to attract the largest audience.

Product placement- The process by which manufacturers or advertisers pay a fee in order for branded products to be prominently displayed in a movie, TV show, or other media production

Soundbite- A short clip of speech or music extracted from a longer piece of audio, often used to promote or exemplify the full-length piece

Talent coordinator- Person who handles details of booking talent as requested by the media outlet

ABOUT THE AUTHOR

Michelby Whitehead began her media career as an undergraduate at Nicholls State University in Thibodaux, LA. Her first "proud moment in PR" was media training a client for the Oprah Winfrey talk show. After graduating in 2008, she became employed in New Orleans at the national headquarters of ACORN (Association for Community Organizations for Reform Now) where she served as its online communication coordinator.

Eventually, the organization dissolved all its U.S. offices, and Michelby found herself unemployed. Refusing to let her degree and her passion for communications go to waste, she began to build her brand as a publicist while working in elementary, secondary, and higher education. In 2013, she was able to pursue entrepreneurship full-time and live life on her own terms. With clients ranging from reality TV stars to fashion designers, medical professionals, business influencers, and

Hollywood executives, Michelby is the plug for entrepreneurs who want publicity like an A-list celeb.

Reaching back to help undergraduates is a core part of Michelby's brand. She has been invited to speak at Howard, Grambling, and the University of Louisiana at Lafayette, sharing her expertise as a panelist and workshop facilitator.

Journalism is an extension of her love for media. Michelby has written for popular digital publications such as Madame Noire, Xo Necole, Curly Nikki, and Grind Pretty, and served as the Creative Director for Koereyelle's *Werk Mag*.

In addition to this, she is an active For(bes) the Culture member, moderating panels and serving as a mentor for its startup cohort.

To work with Michelby in any capacity, contact hello@michelby.com !

TOOLS YOU CAN USE

To help you pitch more effectively, I've included a 12-month Press Goals workbook at the end of *Write on Time!* But that's not all...

As a token of appreciation, I'm offering the **PitchHER Perfect Publicity Kit™** for **FREE**! It contains all the tools you need to position your expertise and brand for media exposure. It includes a Public Relations Plan, Press Release, Media Kit, and a Pitch or Ditch Guide!

Leave an Amazon review on how *Write on Time!* has helped you. Next, email a screenshot of your review to hello@michelby.com, and the PitcHER Perfect Publicity Kit™ is all yours!

January Press Goals

PITCH ANGLES:

NATIONAL OUTLETS:

LOCAL OUTLETS:

CONTACT INFO:

MY DEADLINE TO SEND PITCH:

February Press Goals

PITCH ANGLES:

NATIONAL OUTLETS:

LOCAL OUTLETS:

CONTACT INFO:

MY DEADLINE TO SEND PITCH:

March Press Goals

PITCH ANGLES:

NATIONAL OUTLETS:

LOCAL OUTLETS:

CONTACT INFO:

MY DEADLINE TO SEND PITCH:

April Press Goals

PITCH ANGLES:

NATIONAL OUTLETS:

LOCAL OUTLETS:

CONTACT INFO:

MY DEADLINE TO SEND PITCH:

May Press Goals

PITCH ANGLES:

NATIONAL OUTLETS:

LOCAL OUTLETS:

CONTACT INFO:

MY DEADLINE TO SEND PITCH:

June Press Goals

PITCH ANGLES:

NATIONAL OUTLETS:

LOCAL OUTLETS:

CONTACT INFO:

MY DEADLINE TO SEND PITCH:

July Press Goals

PITCH ANGLES:

NATIONAL OUTLETS:

LOCAL OUTLETS:

CONTACT INFO:

MY DEADLINE TO SEND PITCH:

August Press Goals

PITCH ANGLES:

NATIONAL OUTLETS:

LOCAL OUTLETS:

CONTACT INFO:

MY DEADLINE TO SEND PITCH:

September Press Goals

PITCH ANGLES:

NATIONAL OUTLETS:

LOCAL OUTLETS:

CONTACT INFO:

MY DEADLINE TO SEND PITCH:

October Press Goals

PITCH ANGLES:

NATIONAL OUTLETS:

LOCAL OUTLETS:

CONTACT INFO:

MY DEADLINE TO SEND PITCH:

November Press Goals

PITCH ANGLES:

NATIONAL OUTLETS:

LOCAL OUTLETS:

CONTACT INFO:

MY DEADLINE TO SEND PITCH:

December Press Goals

PITCH ANGLES:

NATIONAL OUTLETS:

LOCAL OUTLETS:

CONTACT INFO:

MY DEADLINE TO SEND PITCH:

www.ingramcontent.com/pod-product-compliance
Lightning Source LLC
Chambersburg PA
CBHW071413290426
44108CB00014B/1805